T0272713

www.ingramcontent.com/pod-product-compliance
Lightning Source LLC
Jackson TN
JSHW052139131224
75386JS00039B/1304

YISRAEL ARTZAYNU

OUR HOME,
OUR HOMELAND

יִשְׂרָאֵל אַרְצֵנוּ

Joan L. Florsheim

With Additional Activities by
Marji Gold-Vukson

A.R.E. PUBLISHING, INC.
Denver, Colorado

Shalom. My name is Alon. I live in Haifa. Haifa is a city in the northern part of Israel. My parents came to Israel from the United States after they finished college.

I am a sabra. A sabra is someone who was born in Israel. "Sabra" is also the name of a cactus fruit. It is tough on the outside, but soft and sweet on the inside, just like many native Israelis.

Israel is a small country. I have been to most of its cities and villages. I want you to meet my Israeli friends. They come from all over the country. They will tell you about themselves. They will tell you about our wonderful Homeland. Israel is *your* Homeland, too.

ALON

Boker tov. Good morning! I'm Shmuel. I live in the beautiful Old City of Jerusalem. My great grandparents came to Israel from Poland in the 1920s. They came to get away from people who hated Jews. My family is Modern Orthodox. Our community is very close. Together, we follow all of the holidays and customs in keeping with Jewish law. I might be a Rabbi someday. Right now, though, I love to play soccer. (We call it football here.) I'm a pretty good goalie.

MICHAL

SHMUEL

Hi. My name is Michal. My grandparents lived through the Holocaust in Germany. They came to Israel in 1947. The area was then called Palestine. One year later, Israel became a nation. I am proud that my family helped create our country. I live on a *kibbutz* in the Negev. The Negev is in the south of Israel. There are many boys and girls my age on the *kibbutz*. We work in the *refet* (cattle barn). We go to school. We spend our free time together.

YAEL

Shalom. My name is Yael. I live in a fairly new neighborhood. It is in West Jerusalem. My parents came to Israel from South Africa when I was just a little kid. My father is a doctor. My mother is an artist. I love to paint and to create things with my hands. I hope that one day I will be a well-known artist like my mom.

OREN

Did you ever hear of Rishon Le-Zion? That's okay. Most people haven't. It's a farming community south of Tel Aviv. **My name is Oren.** My grand-parents and great-grandparents came from Yemen in 1949. About 50,000 Yemenite Jews came to Israel in a famous airlift. It was called "Operation Magic Carpet." The people didn't *really* fly on a magic carpet. They flew on El Al (Israel's airline). My father was a member of the Knesset. The Knesset is the parliament of Israel. I have special feelings for the Knesset building in Jerusalem. I also like to visit the archaeology exhibits at the Israel Museum.

RONIT

IBRAHIM

Call me Ronit. My name means "happy one." The name fits me! I have lots of energy and I'm always laughing. My mother made *aliyah* (came to Israel) from Canada. My father came from Russia. They met when they were in the army. They got married when they finished their army service. We live in Tel Aviv. Later, I'll tell you more about this exciting city. I'm going to be a fashion designer or a model when I grow up.

Salaam. That's how we say *shalom* in Arabic. **I'm Ibrahim.** I'm a Christian Arab. My mother, father, four brothers, and I live in a small Arab village in the northern part of Israel. It is near Tiberias. I met Alon last summer at a camp for Jewish and Arab children. We enjoy talking together and playing basketball. I'm glad Alon introduced me to the kids you just met — Michal, Shmuel, Yael, Oren, and Ronit. I'm very shy. I probably would not have met them on my own. Now they are my friends, too. I want to be a teacher when I grow up.

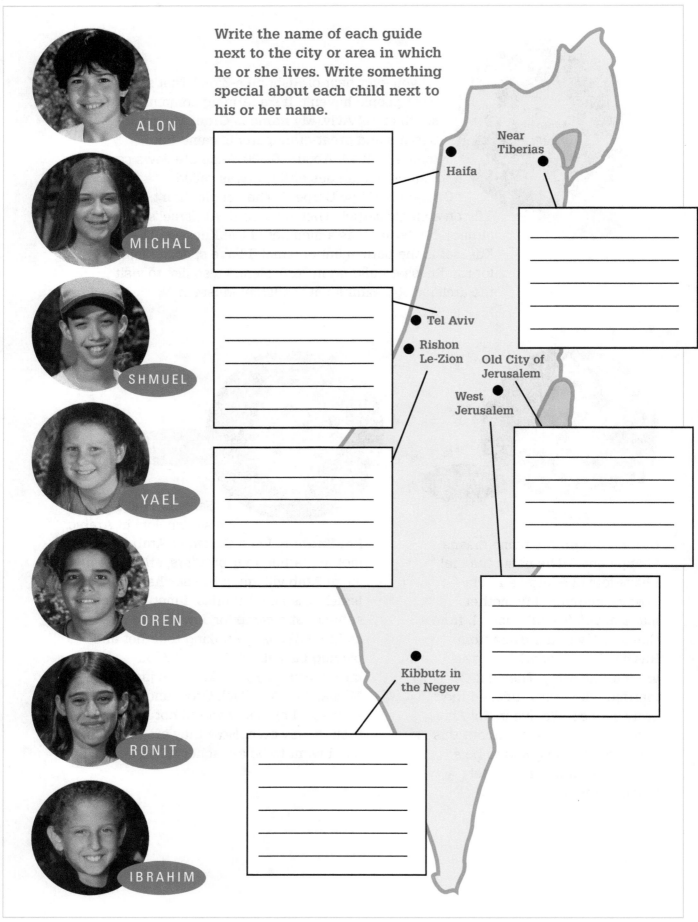

Write the name of each guide next to the city or area in which he or she lives. Write something special about each child next to his or her name.

ALON

MICHAL

SHMUEL

YAEL

OREN

RONIT

IBRAHIM

Near Tiberias

Haifa

Tel Aviv

Rishon Le-Zion

Old City of Jerusalem

West Jerusalem

Kibbutz in the Negev

Now you have met some of my friends. We will be your guides on a special tour of Israel, past and present. Our country is a very unusual place. It is the Jewish Homeland. Millions of Jews actually live here. It is also a home for all Jews who live elsewhere. You'll see what I mean after you have been on our tour.

The State of Israel is very young compared to most countries. We became a country on May 14, 1948 (Iyar 5, 5708 on the Jewish calendar). Our country is young, but our history is very old. Are you surprised to learn that the name Israel is almost 4000 years old . . . and that Jews have lived in this land all of that time?

ALON

How old is the State of Israel now? _____

Suppose you were in Israel in 1948.
Write a birth announcement for the brand new state.

Youngster's Name:

Eretz Yisrael
_____

Date of Birth:
_____

Length (from top to bottom):
_____

Width (at the widest point):
_____

How would you fill in these lines?

Parents:
_____ and _____

Why did you choose whom you did?

_____

Draw a picture or paste a photo of the new little state here:

ALON

Our story is told in the Torah. The Torah tells us that God sent Abraham on a long trip. Abraham came to this land. God promised that he and his people would be given this land forever. Many years later, Abraham's grandson, Jacob, had a dream. In the dream, God told Jacob that his children and their children would always live in the land. God also said that his family would grow and grow. God told Jacob that they would move to many places in the world, but they would always come back to the land.

What did God promise Abraham? _____

Did God's promise come true? _____

Do all promises come true? _____

If someone makes you a promise, do you expect them to

follow through with it? _____

How do you feel if they disappoint you? _____

Do you always follow through on your promises? _____

What do you think? Should promises always be kept? Write YES or NO: _____

List five reasons people *should always* keep their promises.
Example: Others will trust you more if you stick to your word.

1. _____
2. _____
3. _____
4. _____
5. _____

List five reasons people should *not* always keep their promises.
Example: Sometimes things change after you make your promise.
They make your promise seem silly.

1. _____
2. _____
3. _____
4. _____
5. _____

Write a haiku poem to tell what might happen if everyone felt the same way about promises as you do.

_____

_____

_____

Do you know what else happened to Jacob? He wrestled with a stranger who might have been an angel! Jacob was winning. The stranger asked him to let go. Jacob asked for a blessing in return. So the stranger changed Jacob's name to "Israel." Israel means "one who has wrestled with God." The Jewish people are called B'nai Yisrael. We are the children of Jacob, who became Israel. We call our Homeland Israel, too.

In what way was Jacob's new name a blessing?

_____

_____

_____

For hundreds of years, Jewish kings ruled in Israel. For hundreds of years, Jewish prophets spoke about what God wanted the people to do. Our people fought against the Greeks and Romans to protect our religion and our country. So you see, we have been here for a very long time.

ALON

7

ALON

Jews have also lived in other lands. They always hoped to return one day to their Homeland. About 100 years ago, Jews began to arrive here in great numbers. They were trying to get away from the bad treatment of the rulers in Russia.

Pretend that the year is 1919. Soon, you and your family will be moving from Russia to Palestine. The journey will be long and hard. Life in Palestine will be very different from life in Russia. What will your family bring to your new home?

We will bring:

_____ _____ _____

_____ _____ _____

_____ _____ _____

_____ _____ _____

Oh, no! Space on the ship (or train) is very limited! You have too many items for the trip! Circle the five things on your list that are the most important to your family. Below, tell why each one is so important.

Item: It is important to my family because:

1. _____   _____

2. _____   _____

3. _____   _____

4. _____   _____

5. _____   _____

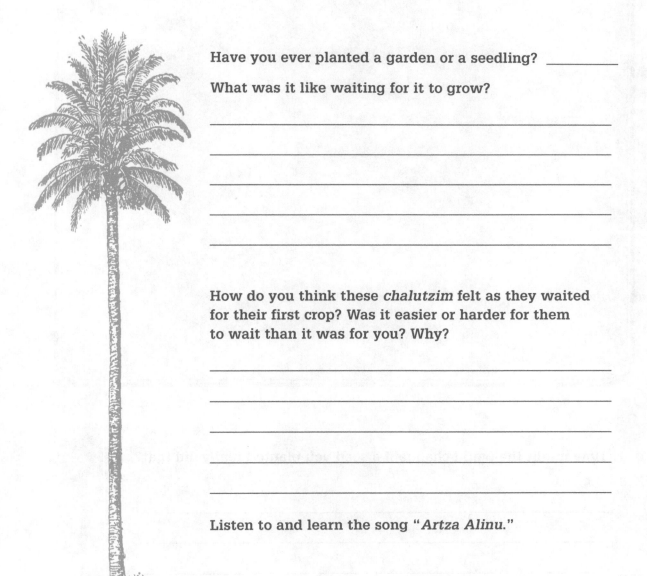

These early settlers were called *chalutzim*. They were young. They dreamed of farming the land that God promised to Abraham, Jacob, and the children of Israel. But in Europe, they lived in cities. They had not worked on farms before.

After a hard day, the *chalutzim* sat around the campfire. They sang about their work. The song "*Artza Alinu*" tells about plowing the land, sowing the seeds, and waiting to harvest the crop.

MICHAL

Have you ever planted a garden or a seedling? _____

What was it like waiting for it to grow?

_____

_____

_____

_____

How do you think these *chalutzim* felt as they waited for their first crop? Was it easier or harder for them to wait than it was for you? Why?

_____

_____

_____

_____

Listen to and learn the song "*Artza Alinu*."

9

What if you planted a magic seed in Israel . . . and it grew into something very strange? In the space below, draw a picture or write a few sentences to tell what grew from your special seed.

How might the world change if a seed you planted *really* did that?

_____

_____

_____

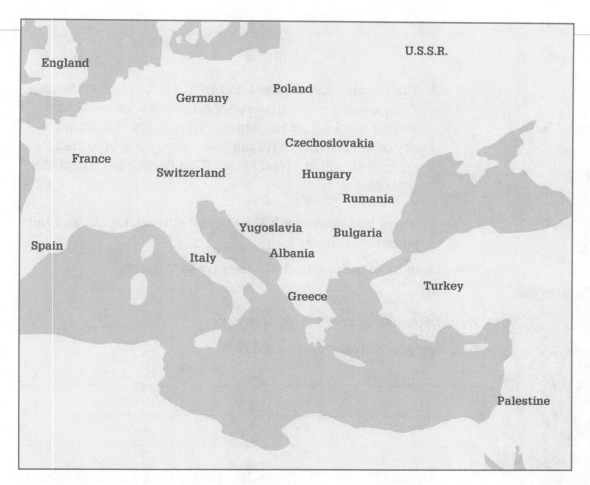

England
U.S.S.R.
Poland
Germany
France
Czechoslovakia
Switzerland
Hungary
Rumania
Spain
Yugoslavia
Bulgaria
Italy
Albania
Greece
Turkey
Palestine

Over the years, many groups of Jews came from other places to live in Palestine. These people were called *olim*. Each group of *olim* was called an Aliyah. (This is Hebrew for "going up." It means moving to Israel.)

Can you think of another time the word "aliyah" is used? How is that like "going up"?

_____

_____

The First Aliyah (1882-1903): These young Jews came from Eastern Europe. They dreamed of working on the land. They had not been farmers, though. They struggled with swamps. They fought mosquitoes that carried disease. They dealt with unfriendly Arab neighbors. Many died or went back home.

What are some things you might have done to survive such a hard life?

_____

_____

The Second Aliyah (1904-1914): These Jews from Eastern Europe were more prepared than the first group. They started the *kibbutz* movement. They began building the city of Tel Aviv. This Aliyah created a group of armed watchmen called "*Hashomer*" (The Guard) to protect their settlements.

If you had come with the Second Aliyah, would you have joined a *kibbutz*? _____

Would you have helped to build the city of Tel Aviv?

_____

Would you have served with *Hashomer*? _____

Tell why you answered as you did.

_____

_____

_____

Third Aliyah (1919-1923): These Jews came from Russia and Poland. They wanted to work their land. They wanted to be friendly neighbors, too. The Arabs were unhappy that more and more Jews were coming. They attacked the Jewish homes and towns. To defend themselves, the Jewish settlers started a military group. It was called the *Haganah*.

Today, every Israeli 18 and older is in the army for two years. Everyone goes back for reserve duty each year. Do you think your country should have the same system? Why or why not?

_____

_____

_____

The Fourth Aliyah (1924-31): These *olim* came to the land to get away from anti-Semitism in Eastern Europe. Anti-Semitism is hatred of Jews. Most of the *olim* settled in the bigger cities. They helped people from preschool through college age go to school. In 1925, they began the Hebrew University on Mount Scopus in Jerusalem. Part of the university is still there today.

Has anyone ever teased you or hurt your feelings because you are Jewish? What could you do if this happened?

_____

_____

The Fifth Aliyah (1932-40): These Jews arrived in Palestine when Hitler rose to power in Germany. This was the largest of all the *Aliyot*. *Aliyot* means more than one *aliyah*. Not all of the European Jews were lucky enough to come, though. The British were in charge of Palestine at that time. They only let a small number of people come in. Many people who stayed in Europe died in the Holocaust.

Ask your parents if any of your relatives lived in Europe during World War II. If so, what happened to them? Share what you find out with the class.

_____

_____

After Israel became a state in 1948, Jews came from all over the world. They came from Europe. They came from many Arab lands, too. In recent years, large groups of *olim* came from Russia, the Former Soviet Union, and Ethiopia. Because Israel welcomes all Jews, these *olim* could come to a country of their own.

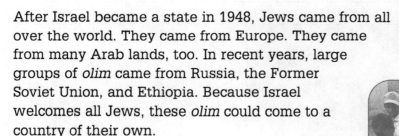

There is a law that allows any Jew to become a citizen of Israel. It is called the Law of Return. Israel can become the home — as well as the Homeland — for all Jews who come to live there.

Why is it important for Israel to have the Law of Return?

_____

_____

Do you know anyone who became an Israeli citizen under the Law of Return? If so, tell your class about it.

MICHAL

My grandparents were lucky. They were able to come to Israel after World War II. They told me many stories about the birth of Israel. The Jews in Palestine wanted their own country. They wanted to be free of British rule. They tried for many years. At last, the United Nations voted to allow Israel to become a country. Jews all over the world were very happy. So were my grandparents! On May 14, 1948, David Ben-Gurion declared Israel's independence. He became Israel's first Prime Minister. Now the settlers had their own country. The large Arab countries near Israel quickly declared war. My grandparents fought in this War of Independence. They wanted to save our tiny, new state. Guess what! Israel won!

Color the map. Use one color for Israel. Use another color for all of her neighbors. What do you notice about this map?

_____

_____

Based on the map, who would have been more likely to win the war?

_____

HOW THE STATE OF ISRAEL WAS BORN

It was in Tel Aviv on Friday, May 14, 1948 (Iyar 5, 5708). At 4 o'clock in the afternoon, just before Shabbat, David Ben-Gurion gave the good news about the new State of Israel. Here are some of the words he said on the radio.

"*Eretz Yisrael was the birthplace of the Jewish people. Here their spiritual, religious, and political identity was shaped. Here they first attained statehood, created cultural values of national and universal significance, and gave to the world the eternal Book of Books . . .*

"*The State of Israel will be open to the immigration of Jews from all countries of their dispersion, will promote the development of the country for the benefit of all its inhabitants; will be based on the precepts of liberty, justice, and peace taught by the Hebrew Prophets . . .*

"*We offer peace and unity to all the neighboring states and their peoples and invite them to cooperate with the independent Jewish nation for the common good of all . . .*"

(Every translation is somewhat different. This one is taken from *Facts about Israel*, published by the Israeli government.)

BUILDERS OF THE STATE

Theodor Herzl was born in 1860. He started the Zionist Movement. Zionism means "love for the land of Israel." Herzl worked very hard to create a new Jewish State. It was sad that he died before his dream came true.

Golda Meir was born in 1898 in Russia. She lived in the United States for a short time. She decided that Palestine was her real home. She moved there when she was a young adult. She was one of the people who created the State of Israel. She held many important positions during her life. She is especially famous as the first and only woman to serve as Prime Minister of Israel.

Chaim Weizmann was born in 1874. He was also one of the creators of Israel. He became the first president. He also began the Weizmann Institute of Science. The research they do there helps the whole world.

MICHAL

Israel won the war, but many Jewish men and women were killed. Some had never held a gun before. Very few had ever been soldiers. Cars and tanks from the War of Independence were left on the road between Ben-Gurion Airport and Jerusalem. They are still there today. They remind us of the brave people who fought for our country.

Were Michal's grandparents trained to be soldiers? _____
Why did they have to fight?

_____

_____

Would you have wanted to fight if you had been in their place?
Why or why not?

_____

_____

What do you think would have happened if young people like Michal's grandparents had not fought for their new country?

_____

_____

_____

Do you think the cars and tanks by the side of the road are a good way to remember the Battle of Jerusalem? _____

What are other ways to remember events such as this?

_____

_____

_____

Sometimes we have to fight, but we would rather live in peace. Pick one of your favorite rhymes. Rewrite it, using different words to tell about peace.

For example, the new words for the rhyme "Row, Row, Row Your Boat" might be:

New Title: A Peaceful Street

**Run, run, run your feet,
quickly down the street!
Give a smile and wave hello,
to everyone you meet.**

Write — and illustrate — your new rhyme here:

New Title: _____

SHMUEL

Jerusalem is our capital. After the war, it was a split city. Jordan ruled over the Old City. They did not let us visit the Temple Mount. They did not let us pray at the *Kotel* (Western Wall). The *Kotel* reminds us of our holy Temple. It is very special to religious Jews like my family.

My grandfather cries with joy when he tells the story about June 6, 1967. Israel was fighting with her Arab neighbors in the Six-Day War. Jordan attacked Israel. Our soldiers entered the Old City and took it back. When they got to the Temple Mount, they blew the shofar. The words on the radio said, "*HaKotel b'yadaynu.*" That means "The *Kotel* is in our hands." The world learned that the *Kotel* was part of the Jewish State again.

When and where is a *shofar* usually blown? Why?

_____

_____

Why do you think that the Israelis blew the *shofar* to tell about their victory at the *Kotel*?

_____

_____

With your classmates, create a newspaper about what happened on June 6, 1967. That was when Jewish soldiers took back the *Kotel*. Here are some ideas for things you might include:

- News stories about what happened
- Poems, cartoons, photographs
- Pretend interviews with people who were there that day
- Editorials that show your own feelings about the events

Get together with your classmates. Put all of the stories, poems, cartoons, photographs, interviews, and editorials together. Make a class newspaper. Don't forget to write a headline for each article. Hang the finished newspaper on a bulletin board for everyone to see.

As soon as the Six-Day War was over, my grandfather bought an apartment. It is in the Old City. He was one of the lucky few who got an apartment there. Our family lives in the same place today. Sometimes I look out from my home at the ancient stones of the *Kotel*. I think I am one of the luckiest boys in the world. It is exciting to live so close to such an important part of our Jewish history.

The *Kotel* is now in Jewish hands. The raised area above the *Kotel* is called the Temple Mount. There are two Muslim holy places of worship on the Mount. Today, the Temple Mount is under Muslim control.

In biblical times, our Temple stood on the Mount. Jews came from all over the land to pray there. The Holy of Holies was a special room in our Temple. The Holy Ark was kept there. Only the High Priest could enter the Holy of Holies. Today, many Orthodox Jews will not go up on the Temple Mount. They are afraid of stepping on the place where the Holy of Holies used to be.

There is a song called "*HaKotel*." The words say that there are men with hearts of stone, but these are stones with hearts of men. What do you think these words mean?

_____

_____

Illustrate what these words mean in the outlines below.

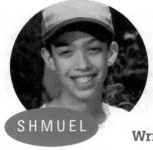

At the *Kotel*, Jews put papers in the openings between the stones. These papers are notes with prayers written on them. We feel we are sending a prayer right to God.

SHMUEL

Write a note to place in the *Kotel*.

Go to <u>www.thewall.org</u> on the Internet. You can see what is happening at the *Kotel* right now. Try this a few times. See what is happening at different times of the day. What do you notice about the *Kotel*?

_____

What do you think the people who pray there feel?

_____

Can you tell who are the "regulars" and who are the first time tourists? _____

What do you notice about where the men and the women are standing?

_____

What emotion did you feel the first time you saw the *Kotel* on the computer in real time? _____

Send a note through the Internet to be put in the *Kotel*.

Today, Israelis and visitors can be seen praying at the *Kotel* any time of day and night. Some Jews go there to see and be near this piece of our religious history. Many boys and girls from Israel and from around the world become Bar or Bat Mitzvah at the *Kotel*. My family likes to go to the *Kotel*. We greet Shabbat there every Friday evening. Many other Israelis and tourists come at the same time.

SHMUEL

What if you were planning to become Bar or Bat Mitzvah at the *Kotel*? List five things you would want to put in your speech about being there at such a special time.

1. _____

2. _____

3. _____

4. _____

5. _____

Tell what your big day at the *Kotel* was like.
Fill in this page from your diary or journal.

Naomi Shemer wrote a song just before the Six-Day War. It is called "*Yerushalayim Shel Zahav.*" The name means "Jerusalem of Gold." It was written when Jordan didn't let Jews into some parts of Jerusalem. The song spoke sadly about not being able to go into the Old City. When the two parts of Jerusalem became one city again, Ms. Shemer wrote another verse. The new verse celebrates the return of the Jews to the Old City. It also tells of the sound of the *shofar* coming from the Temple Mount.

Why is the Temple Mount important?

_____

_____

What is on the Temple Mount now?

_____

_____

Did you ever want something for a long time and then receive it? What was that like?

_____

_____

_____

How do you think the Israelis and Jews around the world felt when they could go back to the *Kotel* after not being able to do so for 19 years?

_____

_____

_____

If these were photos of scenes taken at the Temple Mount and *Kotel*,
what would each picture look like?

1948 C.E.

1967 C.E.

Today

About 2500 C.E.

**What if a new camera let us take a
picture 500 years into the future?
Show what might be going on at the
Temple Mount.**

All buildings in Jerusalem are made of Jerusalem stone. My apartment house is, too. This stone is a light pinkish color, like the sand on a clean beach. When the sun shines on it, it sometimes looks like gold. Jerusalem is now the largest city in our country. The population is more than 650,000. About 450,000 of these are Jews. The rest are Muslims and Christians.

YAEL

Compare the number of people living in your city with the number living in Jerusalem. How many of the people in your city are Jews?

_____

Many kinds of Jews live in Jerusalem. Some, like Shmuel, are *dati* (religious). His family prays every Shabbat. They go to an Orthodox synagogue.

My family is traditional. We also keep many of the *mitzvot* (God's commandments). My family goes to a synagogue, too. It is very much like the Reform or Conservative synagogues where you live.

Most of my friends are secular. They feel very Jewish, but they do not think about religion much. It is easy for them to be Jewish in Israel. Israel is a Jewish state. Israelis live by the Jewish calendar. All of the Jewish holidays are national holidays. The Bible and Jewish history are taught in all Israeli schools.

Why do you think the Bible and Jewish history are taught in Israeli schools?

_____

_____

_____

Would it be easier or harder to be a secular Jew in North America than it would be in Israel? Why?

_____

_____

_____

Is Judaism a religion? _____

Can a person be Jewish without being religious? _____

In Israel, would your family be considered religious,
traditional, secular, or something else?

_____

Pretend that you are a child from a secular family spending a
month visiting your very religious grandparents in Me'ah She'arim.
Or, pretend that you are a child from a very religious family visiting
your secular grandparents in Tel Aviv. What might your trip be like?
What might you write in a letter home?

Dear _____,

Today I got to Saba and Savta's house. Guess what we did!

_____

_____

_____

_____

_____

_____

_____

_____

_____

_____

_____

_____

YAEL

The worship services in Masorti (Conservative) synagogues and Progressive (Reform) synagogues in Israel are much like the ones in your country. The service is usually in Hebrew, though. Why do you think this is so? (Here is a hint: What languages would be spoken in a synagogue in France? What would be spoken in Mexico?)

_____

Children in Israel study for their Bar and Bat Mitzvah just like boys and girls in North America do. How would their studies be different from yours? (Hint: What do they already know that you might have to learn?)

_____

_____

Most Israelis who are not Orthodox are secular. They are Jewish, but they do not go to synagogue. However, the Masorti and Progressive (Reform) groups are growing. They are building synagogues. They are reaching out to Israelis who are looking for a modern way to practice Judaism.

Help someone who can't read English learn how to celebrate Shabbat. You may use pictures, arrows, and anything else that might help the person get the idea.

Without drawing or writing, how might you explain Shabbat to someone who doesn't know your language?

_____

_____

YAEL

Our stores have lots of things from North America. I love Levi jeans. I love Speedo bathing suits. I also like everything in ToysRUs! I like to shop and have lunch with my friends. Sometimes we eat falafel or shwarma. Sometimes we go to MacDonald's for a hamburger. KFC and Pizza Hut are other restaurants we like. Can you believe it? In Israel almost all of these are kosher!

Are all of the restaurants in your city kosher? _____

Are any of them kosher? _____

McDonald's, Pizza Hut, and KFC are kosher only in Israel.

Why do you think this is so? _____

_____

_____

What are the differences between kosher and

non-kosher food at these restaurants? _____

_____

_____

_____

Create a kosher menu for one of these restaurants.
Draw pictures of some of the food choices on your menu.

These restaurants are in downtown Jerusalem.
Circle the ones that are in your city.

McDonald's   **Dunkin' Donuts**   **Chagall**

Melech Hafelafel   **Burger King**   **Pizza Hut**

The Yemenite Step

Make up a name for a restaurant that features each of these
other popular Israeli foods. Example: Nosh So Fast!

Food:	Name of Restaurant:
Ice cream	_____
Donuts	_____
Olives	_____
Pomegranates	_____
Sea Bass	_____
Steaks	_____

Pick your favorite restaurant name from the lists above. Design a sign for it.

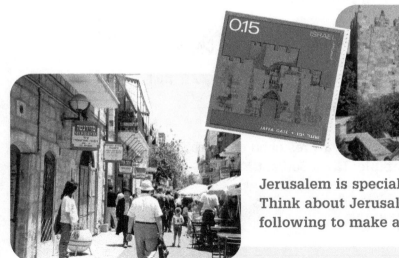

Jerusalem is special for many people. Think about Jerusalem. Then fill in the following to make an acrostic poem:

J is for _____.

E is for _____.

R is for _____.

U is for _____.

S is for _____.

A is for _____.

L is for _____.

E is for _____.

M is for _____.

Archaeologists are people who dig in the earth. They find objects that help us know how people lived many years ago. Some of the things they find were used or worn long, long ago. Archaeology is a hobby for many Israelis. It is also my hobby.

OREN

Suppose your family is moving to a new home. The movers take everything to your new house. Almost. Something is left behind in the garden. As time goes by, it gets covered with dirt. Years later, the archaeologists get to work. They are like detectives. They look at the things you left behind. Then they can guess how your family lived. They imagine what kind of dishes and tools you used. They figure out what your clothes looked like and what you ate. They can tell a lot even from a tiny seed.

Pretend that this is the year 3200. An archaeologist is digging in the place where your house once stood. She finds a piece of a *Seder* plate you made in preschool. She finds a metal pan, a baby bottle, and a soda can.

What other things might she find that your family left behind?

_____   _____

_____   _____

_____   _____

_____   _____

List some things she might learn about your life from the things she found.

_____

_____

_____

_____

_____

One of my favorite places in Jerusalem is the Israel Museum. There are lots of artifacts (very old objects) there. They were found by archaeologists. Some of the pottery is thousands of years old. A few pieces were found almost whole. Others have been carefully glued together like a jigsaw puzzle.

 OREN

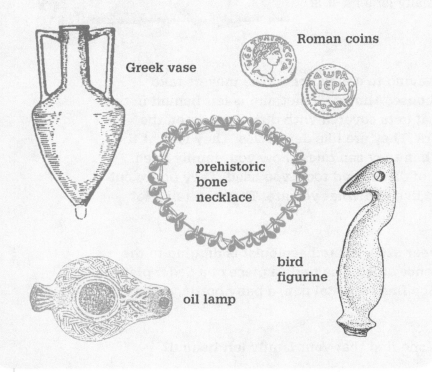

Greek vase

Roman coins

prehistoric
bone
necklace

bird
figurine

oil lamp

In Israel, archaeology can be a hobby. It is also an important job. There are many artifacts waiting to be found. These were left by many groups of people. They lived in the area long ago. The Orthodox Jews are worried. They are afraid that people might dig where Jews are buried. That would be against Jewish law. Sometimes, digging has to stop because of this.

Choose one of the artifacts in the picture.

Which one did you choose? _____

What was the object used for?

_____

How many other things could you do with that object today?
Think of many different and unusual uses. Write them here.

_____

_____

_____

_____

_____

I want to be an artist. I go to the Israel Museum, too. My favorite things to see there are the paintings and sculptures. They are by Israelis and artists from other countries. I also enjoy the beautiful Jewish ritual objects and clothing from around the world. There are even parts of lovely old synagogues from other countries where Jews lived.

YAEL

Pretend that you are a famous artist. Israel has asked you to design a special postage stamp celebrating the Israel Museum. Show what your stamp would look like.

Tell why you chose the design you did.

_____

_____

_____

The Billy Rose Art Garden is my favorite part of the museum. The sculptures are great. I especially like the one by Robert Indiana. It spells out the Hebrew word for love. That word is אהבה (ahavah). It's fun to climb up on the art. From there I can look out over my city.

YAEL

In the space below, design your own sculpture about *ahavah*. Then make it out of clay or other things.

 OREN

Part of the Hebrew University is on the top of a mountain. The mountain is in East Jerusalem. It is called Mount Scopus. From here, you can see the Old City of Jerusalem. You can see where King David built his capital more than 3,000 years ago.

Here are some people looking over the city of Jerusalem from Mount Scopus. What is each person thinking?

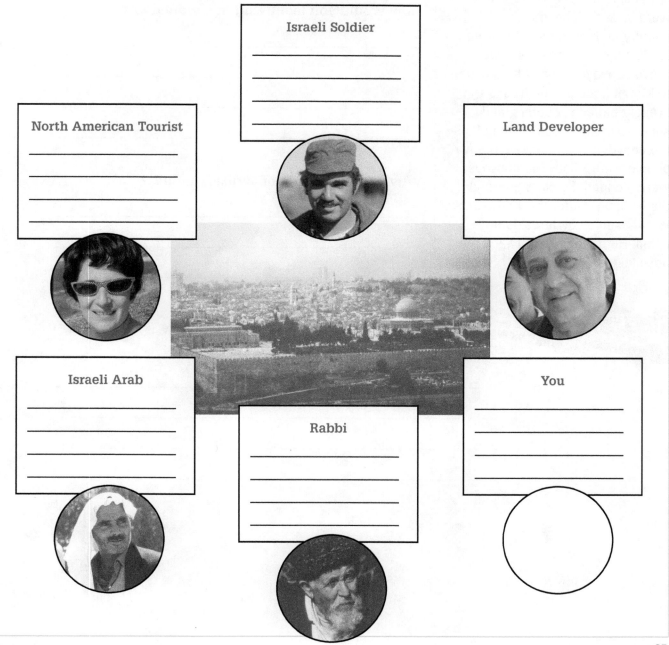

Israeli Soldier

_____
_____
_____

North American Tourist

_____
_____
_____

Land Developer

_____
_____
_____

Israeli Arab

_____
_____
_____

Rabbi

_____
_____
_____

You

_____
_____
_____

Tall walls go all the way around the Old City. These have been built and rebuilt several times over the years. The walls protected the people who lived inside them.

The Hebrew University and Hadassah Hospital are on Mount Scopus. From 1948 to 1967, they were in Jewish hands. The country of Jordan ruled the area leading up to them. At first, Jews drove convoys (lines of trucks) up to Mount Scopus. The trucks brought patients, doctors, and supplies to the hospital. One of the convoys was attacked. Many people were killed. The convoys were stopped. Soldiers guarded the buildings. After the 1967 war, Israel ruled all of Jerusalem again. Both the university and the hospital were rebuilt.

How would you feel living in a walled city?

_____

_____

_____

_____

Why were the walls of Jerusalem built?

_____

_____

_____

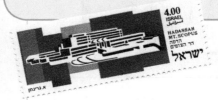

Why do you think that at a later time people began to live outside of the walls?

_____

_____

_____

_____

There is a monster in West Jerusalem! It's called the "*Mifletzet*." It's not a real monster. It's a big red sculpture with many red tongues to slide down. Sometimes, I picnic nearby. I like to watch kids having fun sliding down my monster's tongues.

YAEL

Compare the *Mifletzet* with the slides in your favorite playground.
Do you think you and your friends would like to play on the Mifletzet?

_____

What is your favorite type of outdoor play?

_____

Boys and girls in Israel love splashing at water parks and hiking.
Would you enjoy doing that? Tell your classmates about a visit to a
water park or about a hike you took.

_____

_____

_____

Write a commercial asking children to come and play on the Mifletzet.

RONIT

Tel Aviv is a big, modern city. It is built on sand dunes on the shores of the Mediterranean Sea. It has office buildings and stores. It has many things to do. The first buildings were put up there about a hundred years ago. I'm proud that Tel Aviv was the first all-Jewish city anywhere in the world. Yaffo is an old seaport. In 1950, Yaffo joined with Tel Aviv. They became one city. Tel Aviv-Yaffo is the second largest city in Israel.

There is a lot to do in Tel Aviv! Our family loves to go to concerts and plays. In good weather, we all like to sit in a café. We watch the people

going by. My older brother and his girlfriend enjoy dancing at the discos. Discos stay open very late at night. I can't wait to do that! My *Ima* (Mom) says that the shopping in Tel Aviv is great. My *Abba* (Dad) loves the excitement of the city, which is lively all day and all night. He is a computer programmer. He works for one of the many hi-tech companies near Tel Aviv.

Look up information about Tel Aviv on the Internet. Make a list of facts about Tel Aviv. Find some information about the many outdoor markets in the Tel Aviv-Yaffo area. They sell everything from food and clothing to antiques and crafts.

A *shuk* is an outdoor market. With your classmates, set up a *shuk* in your classroom. Ask your parents for one or two items from home to sell. Give the money you raise to a *tzedakah* project in Israel.

Here are some things to see in Tel Aviv:

- See the Mediterranean Sea. Its beaches are full of people playing and swimming.
- See the "*tayelet.*" It is a promenade with crowds of people walking, shopping, and eating.
- See David Ben-Gurion's home. It has a huge library.
- See Bayt Bialik. It is the home of Chaim Nachman Bialik, Israel's most famous poet.

What are three things in Tel Aviv-Yaffo that remind you of a North American city you know?

_____

_____

_____

What are three things that are different from the cities you know?

_____

_____

_____

What would you most like to see in Tel Aviv-Yaffo?

_____

_____

Think about Tel Aviv-Yaffo and Jerusalem.
How are these cities alike? How are they different?

_____

_____

_____

Yaffo is one of the oldest cities in Israel. The Book of Jonah in the Bible calls it a port city. Some of the first *olim* arrived through this port. Yaffo also has a new area. It is an artist colony. There are many art galleries. There are also wonderful nightclubs and restaurants. The streets are narrow and hilly. The buildings are very old. Most have been remodeled. They are beautiful inside.

Design an official shield for the artist colony of Yaffo. The design should tell at least five things about the city.

Explain how the things in your shield design tell about Yaffo.

I like to go to the beach with my family. We go on Shabbat and holidays. Shabbat is the only day of the week that my parents do not have to work. They work from Sunday through Thursday. Most people do not work at all on Fridays. My father has to work in the morning. On Friday, everybody gets home by early afternoon. We get ready for Shabbat. On Shabbat, we all stay together. I love Shabbat because it is a special family time.

Like many Israelis, Ronit and her family are not religious. They even go to the beach on Shabbat.
What are some of the special things that you like to do with your family on Shabbat?

_____

_____

_____

_____

Get together with a few classmates. Write a skit that shows different ways a family could spend a special Shabbat together. Examples: long walks in the neighborhood, act out the Torah portion, visit family.

Pretend that you were in Israel on Shabbat. Use your senses to think of many different and unusual things you might see, taste, touch, hear, and smell.

I might see:

I might taste:

I might touch:

I might hear:

I might smell:

Tel Aviv has a great museum. It is called Beth Hatefutsoth. It is the Museum of the Diaspora. (The diaspora is every place in the world outside of Israel where Jews live or have lived.)

RONIT

The museum is such a special place. There, you can learn about lots of synagogues. They are from all over the world. There are also videos of many Jewish communities. The displays show how Jews have lived. They show how Jews have kept the Jewish spirit alive.

When you go into the museum, you see slides of Jewish faces. These are the faces of Jews from all over the world.

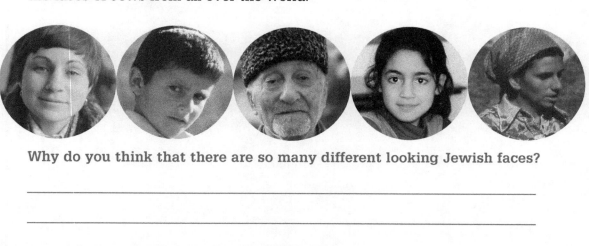

Why do you think that there are so many different looking Jewish faces?

_____

_____

Where might these Jews have come from?

_____

_____

Which face looks most like you?

_____

Do you have friends from different countries?
Do they look the same as you? Do they look different from you?
Explain your answer.

_____

_____

_____

Design a new display for Beth Hatefutsoth. It should be all about Jewish life in your community. As you plan, find out about:

- the history of your Jewish community
- what the community is like today
- the groups and activities in your Jewish community
- synagogues in your area
- other interesting information

Describe — or draw and label — what your display would include.

What is the main thing people who see your display will learn about your Jewish community?

_____

_____

Would you like to see pictures of the faces from the museum slide show? You can! Learn more about Beth Hatefutsoth on the Internet.
Ask your teacher or parent to help you visit the site. Have fun!

People use the museum computers to learn about lots of things. They learn about places where Jews lived in the past. They learn where Jews are living today. They use the computers to trace their family's name.

Ask your parents to help you learn about your family tree. See how many relatives you can trace. On the chart below, write the names of your ancestors. If you can, write down where each of them lived. You and your classmates can show each family's journey on a map of the world.

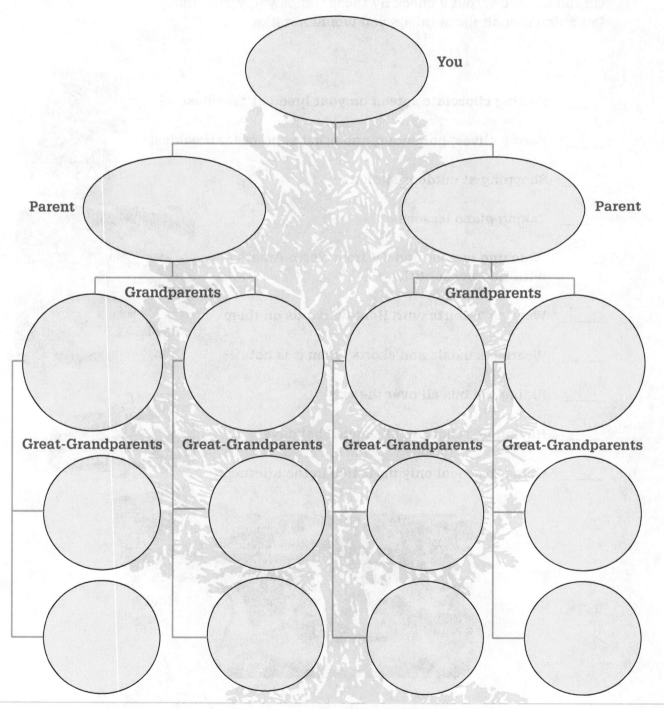

You

Parent

Parent

Grandparents

Grandparents

Great-Grandparents   Great-Grandparents   Great-Grandparents   Great-Grandparents

RONIT

Many of our Israeli foods and activities are the same as yours. Some are different.

On the list below, put a check by those things you would like. Put a line though those things you would not like.

_____ Putting chocolate spread on your bread at breakfast

_____ Eating olives, hummous, and other veggies for breakfast

_____ Shopping at outdoor markets

_____ Taking piano lessons

_____ Watching movies and TV from North America with Hebrew subtitles

_____ Wearing T-shirts with Hebrew words on them

_____ Wearing sandals and shorts when it is hot

_____ Riding the bus all over the city

_____ Having no school on all Jewish holidays

_____ Going to school only until 1:00 in the afternoon

There are many types of schools in Israel. I go to a state school. Our classes are a lot like yours. We study science, math, spelling, and history. Everything is taught in Hebrew. We also study Hebrew, English, Bible, and Jewish history. There are other kinds of schools, too.

RONIT

Some are TALI schools. These are public schools, too. They teach about Jewish customs and ways.

Some are state religious schools. These schools are for Modern Orthodox students. They are for kids who want to learn about traditional Judaism. Shmuel goes to a state religious school.

Others are *yeshivot*. These schools are for ultra-Orthodox students. They mostly study Jewish subjects. Many of these students do not go to college. They go on to study at higher-level *yeshivot* instead.

Which of these schools is most like yours?

_____

What subjects do Israeli students study that you do not?

_____

_____

_____

What subjects do you have in school that Israeli students do not?

_____

_____

_____

What would your dream school be like?

_____

_____

_____

What classes would be taught at your dream school?
Add your own ideas to the examples below.

horseback Frisbee   scuba diving Eilat-style
ice cream technology   ancient history
creative writing   comic book production

_____   _____

_____   _____

_____   _____

_____   _____

What special training would the teachers have?

_____

_____

What would the school look like? Show it below.
Label the most important parts.

ALON

My city is Haifa. It is a port city on the Mediterranean Sea. Haifa is the third largest city in Israel. Tankers bring oil to the huge oil refinery here. Other ships bring steel and lumber.

Outgoing ships take beautiful Israeli fruits, vegetables, and flowers to other countries. You may have seen some of them in your stores.

Design a series of postcards. Show some of the produce that is sent from Haifa. Oranges, peaches, avocados, watermelons, and grapes are among them. Tomatoes, cucumbers, and green peppers are, too.

ALON

Haifa is built on the steep slopes of Mount Carmel. It has a lot of hills. It reminds some people of San Francisco. The buildings are on three levels. My house is built right into the hillside. It is on the second level. I take a little subway up the mountain to my house. The subway is called the Carmelit. At the very top of the mountain is a national park.

There is a world famous university in Haifa. It is called the Technion. Engineering, advanced sciences, and hi-tech subjects are taught here. Great scientific research is done here, too.

What do you think is the biggest problem in the world today?

_____

_____

Pretend that you are a student at the Technion.
You have come up with a high-tech invention.
It will help solve the problem! Show it here. Label the parts.

Tell how your idea would help solve the world's biggest problem.

I am an Israeli Arab. My family lives in an Arab village. It is near Tiberias. We are Israeli citizens. Most of the Arabs in Israel are Muslim. My family is Christian. My parents work in a modern hotel. It is on the shores of the Kinneret. This large lake is also called the Sea of Galilee. We like living in the northern part of Israel. We are close to many places that are important to us as Christians.

IBRAHIM

My brothers and I love the Kinneret. We swim, waterski, and boat. We can catch delicious St. Peter's fish. We also like to explore the historical sites. There are some very old baths here. They were built by the Romans over natural hot springs. This is a great place to live or to visit.

Do you enjoy swimming? _____

Have you ever been waterskiing or boating or fishing?

_____

Where do you go now to do these things?

_____

Would you like to go to the Kinneret someday and do them there?

_____

The downtown area of Tiberias is always very busy. It is right on the Kinneret. A short distance away, the lake is quiet and peaceful. Some of the early *chalutzim* settled nearby. It is easy to see why they loved this lake.

Pretend that you are a travel agent. Plan a trip for a client who wants to visit Tiberias and the Kinneret. Fill in the sheet below. Help your client learn more about the area.

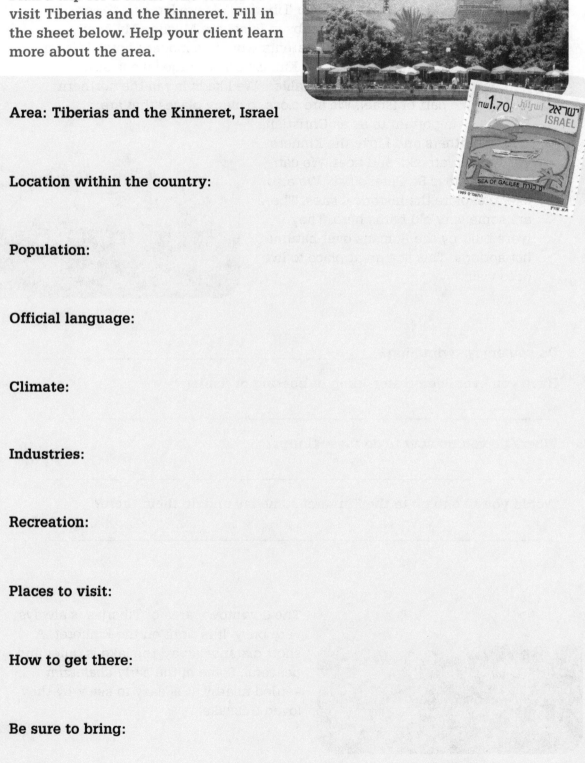

Area: Tiberias and the Kinneret, Israel

Location within the country:

Population:

Official language:

Climate:

Industries:

Recreation:

Places to visit:

How to get there:

Be sure to bring:

The poet Rachel was one of the early *chalutzim*. She loved the Kinneret and the land around it. She wrote many poems about it. Some of them are very serious. Some are sad. You can tell that she had deep feelings for this part of Israel. She is buried near the shore of the Kinneret. People sit by her grave and read her poems.

Why do you think people read Rachel's poetry by her grave?

_____

_____

Why do you think some of the early *chalutzim* chose an area like Tiberias to start to build the country?

_____

_____

Write a poem about a special place that you love.
The poem can be happy or serious.

Remember me? I'm the artist in our group of friends. That's why I love the city of Safed. It's an artist colony. Safed is high in the hills. It is in the Galilee in the north of Israel. It's not too far from where Ibrahim lives. The old streets are very narrow. I hope one day to make beautiful pieces of art like the ones in Safed.

YAEL

I also like to visit the tiny old synagogues in Safed. Many are more than 400 years old. My friend Shmuel once went with me to Safed. He told me about the famous Rabbis and wise teachers who used to live there. Some of the synagogues are named after them.

The Rabbis and teachers of Safed taught us to think of the Sabbath eve as a Bride. They welcomed her each week with song and dance.

How would you welcome the Sabbath Bride?
Write your very own prayer welcoming her. You may look in a Siddur for ideas.

I know another great place for a vacation. It is the beautiful resort city of Eilat. When it's cold in your part of the world, it is sunny and warm there. Eilat is at the southern tip of Israel. It is not far from my *kibbutz*. It's right by the Red Sea. You can see Jordan from the beach. Many tourists go from Eilat to Jordan now that our two countries have made peace.

MICHAL

My family went to Eilat last winter. We snorkeled in the Red Sea. We also rode in a boat. It had a glass bottom. We saw the coral reefs in the water. The aquarium is very special. We saw thousands of fish through glass windows. We stayed dry even though we were below the level of the water.

Have you ever been to an aquarium? If so, tell your classmates about it.

Here is an ad from the *Eilat Times*.

Write a song to tell the story behind the ad.

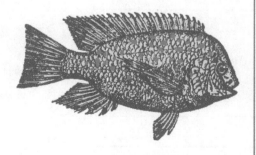

The Song of Dag

SHMUEL

Beersheva is a city even older than Jerusalem. Abraham and Sarah lived here. Isaac, Rebecca, and Jacob all lived here, too. It was Abraham who named the city Beersheva. It means "seven wells."

Beersheva is the capital of the Negev. It is in the far south of Israel. It is the center of activity for the small cities and farming towns near it.

David Ben-Gurion was one of the founders of the Israel. He was Israel's first Prime Minister. He loved the Negev. In fact, he retired there on a *kibbutz*. The *kibbutz* is called S'de Boker. Ben-Gurion University was named after David Ben-Gurion. It is known for studies of the plants and climate of the Negev. It is also known for its medical school.

There is something very colorful in Beersheva. It is the weekly Bedouin market. You can buy a camel or a TV set there. Food, animals, clothing, and laptops are all for sale. You've never seen anything like it!

Suppose you could buy — and take home — five items from the Bedouin market! What would your shopping list look like?

Shuk Shopping

Example: baby camel, 12 to18 months old

1. _____

2. _____

3. _____

4. _____

5. _____

Look at your list. Look at the lists your classmates made.
Which things were on many of the lists? Which things were the most unusual?

_____

_____

Morph into Israel

Here is a fun way to look at and learn about the map of Israel. It will help you remember where the different places are.

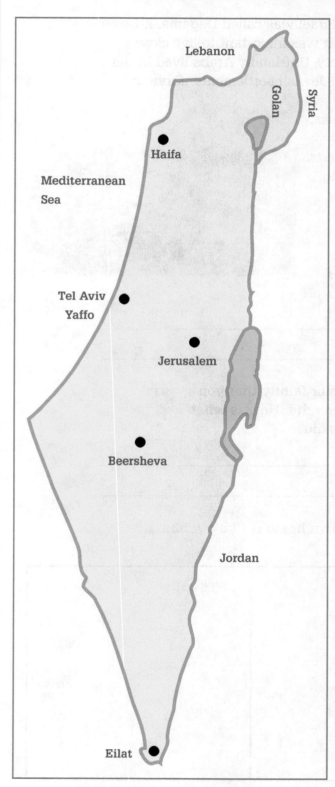

Stand up straight with room to move about. You are about to become the map of Israel!

The belly button of Israel is **Jerusalem**. Place your finger on your belly button. Your center is the Holy City.

Now reach your hands straight above your head. Wave to our Arab neighbors in **Lebanon**. Keep your hands up. Lean to your left and wave to the Arab neighbors in **Syria**. Lower your hands on the left side of your body. You are now waving to the Arabs of **Jordan**.

Move your hands up to your left ear. Cup them around the ear. Listen to the sound of the waters of the **Kinneret**, the **Sea of Galilee**.

Now move your right hand out to the side in a sweeping motion. This is the **Mediterranean Sea**. The port city of **Haifa** is where your shoulder is.

Turn your head to the left. Your face is now the **Golan Heights**. That's way up north. You can ski down **Mount Hermon** from the bridge of your nose.

Return to **Jerusalem** (your belly button). Move your hand to your right waist. **Tel Aviv** and the ancient seaport of **Yaffo** are there.

Now "travel" south. Touch your knees. You are now in **Beersheva**.

Keep going south until you reach your toes. **Eilat** is at the southern tip of Israel.

Do this again. See how fast you can morph into Israel!

There is one type of community found only in Israel. It is the *kibbutz*. A *kibbutz* is a collective farm. This means that the community owns everything on the *kibbutz* together.

The first *kibbutz* in Israel was called Degania. It began in 1909. At that time, it was important to live close to others. This was for safety. Unfriendly Arabs lived in the area. Sometimes they attacked Jewish settlements. *Kibbutz* members guarded their homes.

MICHAL

Kibbutz members are called *kibbutzniks*. They work together as a group.

Kibbutzim means more than one *kibbutz*. The early *kibbutzim* gave houses, clothing, food, and schooling to all who lived there. *Kibbutzim* still do this today.

Why did the early *kibbutzniks* feel safer living on a *kibbutz* than on their own?

_____

_____

Did you ever do something with friends or family that you could not have done alone? Tell what you did. How is what you did like what the early *kibbutzniks* did?

_____

_____

Draw a comic strip to show how your own home is like a *kibbutz*.

On a *kibbutz* everyone has a job. Some people work in the kitchen. Some work in the laundry or chicken house. Others work in the fields or in the office. Everyone works as part of a team. This helps the whole *kibbutz.* *Kibbutzniks* share everything. We even eat our meals together. We eat in the *Chadar Ochel*. That is our dining hall. Each *kibbutz* member is given an allowance.

MICHAL

Years ago, *kibbutz* children lived in "children's houses." They visited their parents only at certain times. Today, children live with their parents. They live in modern apartments. They can eat in their own apartments if they want.

We still do a lot of farming, but we also have a factory. We make plastic items. Other *kibbutzim* have hi-tech industries. We earn some money by running a guest house. It is for tourists. My dad is the manager. I'm sure he'd love to welcome you one day! Some of our members go into the city to work each day. My mother does.

The *kibbutz* movement is much smaller than it used to be. Some of our members chose not to come back to the *kibbutz* after college. They like life in the city. Yet, my family and many others still love the *kibbutz* way of life.

The children lived in special houses away from their families in the early years of the *kibbutz* movement. Why do you think this was done?

_____

_____

_____

_____

Find out what farm products are raised on *kibbutzim* today.
Make a chart of these. Add a drawing of each product.

Write a short story
about living in a
kibbutz children's
house. It should be
from a toddler's point
of view. Include a
photo or drawing.

Many *kibbutzim* are secular. (Think of our non-religious friends in Tel Aviv and Jerusalem.) Some are religious or traditional. Secular *kibbutzim* keep the Jewish holidays. They do it in their own way. They honor them as historic or harvest holidays.

At our *kibbutz*, we love Shavuot. We bring in the first fruits of the harvest. We have a big dinner in the *Chadar Ochel*. We sing and dance. The children act in plays. We sing songs that we learned in school.

MICHAL

Why do you think *kibbutzim* celebrate the harvest?

_____

Make up a song or dance that could be performed at one of these celebrations. Perform it for your classmates.

What if you filled a big paper bag with things for celebrating Shavuot on a *kibbutz*? What would you put in the bag? Why?

I would put:	to tell about:
grapes	the "first fruits" brought to the ancient Temple
_____	_____
_____	_____
_____	_____
_____	_____
_____	_____

Circle each item that you could use for Shavuot only on a *kibbutz*. Do not circle things that would be used for Shavuot off of a *kibbutz*. Look at the example above. "Grapes" could be used at Shavuot both on and off of a *kibbutz*. It is not circled.

What did you find out about celebrating Shavuot?

_____

Shabbat is special in Israel. It is special on the *kibbutz*, too. On weekdays, most *kibbutz* families eat some meals in their own apartment. On Friday evening, everyone gets dressed up. They enjoy dinner in the *Chadar Ochel*. On Shabbat morning, families relax together. They do things they don't have time to do during the workweek.

MICHAL

What might you like to do on Shabbat on a secular *kibbutz*?

_____

_____

_____

With some of your classmates, build a model of a *kibbutz*. Show the farm areas and buildings for business. Make guest houses for tourists and homes for the members. Don't forget an office, a *Chadar Ochel*, and a pool. Barns, animals, orchards, and fields would be great, too. You may add any other things you would like to have on your *kibbutz*.

My cousins live on a *moshav*. That is another kind of farming community. There, every family has its own house and land. Each family works its own fields. All of the families help pay for machines and labor. Like a *kibbutz*, a *moshav* is a close community. *Moshavim* means more than one *moshav*. Some *moshavim* have industry as well as farming.

RONIT

How is a *moshav* like a *kibbutz*? How is it different?

_____

Would you rather live on a *moshav* or a *kibbutz*? Why?

_____

Finish these funny letters between a child living on a *kibbutz* and his or her cousin living on a *moshav*.

Dear Cousin _____,
    Today it was my turn to work in the refet (cattle barn) on our kibbutz. You will never guess what happened!

_____

_____

_____

_____

_____

_____

_____

_____

    Love, _____

Dear Cousin _____,
    You think that's funny? Let me tell you what happened on the moshav!

_____

_____

_____

_____

_____

_____

_____

_____

    Love, _____

I'm proud that Israel is a democracy just like your country. Israel is the only one in the Middle East. U.S. citizens vote for a President. Canadians vote for a Prime Minister. We vote for our Prime Minister. We also vote for the members of the Knesset.

There are many political parties in Israel. Some are made up of Arabs. Some of the Knesset members are Arabs. In the Knesset building, there is a beautiful tapestry. It is by the Jewish artist

Marc Chagall. It shows King David dancing with the Torah. He is entering Jerusalem. King David made Jerusalem the capital of his state. More than 3,000 years later, it is still our capital.

Why do you think Marc Chagall chose King David as the main idea for his tapestry in the Knesset?

_____

_____

_____

Israelis vote for a political party. Each party has a list of people running for office. They are chosen by party members. Suppose a party gets enough votes for three seats in the Knesset. The top three names on their list of people running become members. What if they get more votes? Then more people on their list become members! Another election is held to pick the Prime Minister.

Would you have chosen King David? Why or why not?

_____

_____

_____

_____

_____

What else might have been chosen?

_____

Pretend you have entered a contest to win a week's vacation in Jerusalem. The winner will meet with the Prime Minister. You must write a 200-word essay. It will tell the best and worst things about being the only democracy in the Middle East.

Essay

_____
_____
_____
_____
_____
_____
_____

Pretend you won the trip to Jerusalem! Hooray!
Describe what you will see. Tell what you will do during your week there. What will you discuss with the Prime Minister?

_____
_____
_____
_____
_____
_____
_____
_____

This is a picture of the Israeli symbol of state.

What two things do you see in this symbol?

_____

_____

What do you think these things mean?

_____

_____

Would you have picked the same objects for a symbol?
Why or why not? What other things might you have added?

_____

_____

Draw the Israeli symbol of state. Add other objects that you think are needed. Tell why you added what you did.

I'm sure you have seen our Israeli flag. It is blue and white. It has a Star of David between two stripes. The Star of David is called a *Magen David* in Hebrew.

People gave lots of ideas for the design of the flag. They picked the one that combined the *Magen David* with the look of a *tallit*. A *tallit* is a prayer shawl. The *Magen David* stands for Judaism.

MICHAL

In what ways are a tallit and the Israeli flag like each other?

_____

_____

_____

Tallitot means more than one *tallit*. Today, there are many types of *tallitot*. Design another flag for Israel that could also be used as a *tallit*.

For a long time, Jews could not to leave Russia. They wrote songs about their dreams of going to Israel. One of these was called "Kachol v'Lavan." That means "Blue and White." It calls the Israeli flag "my colors." The flag of Israel meant a lot to Jews who could only dream of living in a free Jewish country.

There is a large *menorah* outside of the Knesset. It has seven branches. It was a gift to Israel from England. Inside the Knesset, the 120 seats are set in the shape of a *menorah*.

 O R E N

Why is the menorah used as a symbol both outside and inside the Knesset?

_____

The *menorah* is first talked about in the Torah. The Israelites were walking in the desert. God told Moses to make a seven-branched *menorah*. It was to be made of pure gold. It would be used in the Tabernacle. That was the worship space in the desert. Today, there is a *menorah* in almost every synagogue. It is in some homes, too. It is not the same as a Chanukah *menorah*. (That is called a *chanukiah* in Hebrew). That one has nine branches.

What does a *menorah* mean to you?
What does it mean to the Jewish people?

_____

_____

A tongue twister is hard to say. It has many of the same sounds. Write a tongue twister about a *menorah*.

How many branches does the *menorah* in front of the Knesset have? _____

How many branches does a *chanukiah* have? _____

Did you ever see a seven-branched menorah? If so, where was it?

_____

68

IBRAHIM

Israel is a Jewish state. About five out of every six people here are Jewish. These Jews come from all over the world. They have many different customs and ways of life. There are also people here with other beliefs. Let me tell you about them. Some of these groups are Christians, Muslims, Druze, and Bedouin.

There are many groups of Christians in Israel. Each group has its own church. Christians share the Church of the Holy Sepulchre in Jerusalem. Some of the Christians are Arabs like me. Some are from Europe or North America. Like the Jews, Christians think of Jerusalem as a holy city. They also call Israel the Holy Land.

Islam is the religion of the Muslims. Muslims call their god Allah. Next to the Jews, the Muslims are the largest religious group in Israel. Almost all of them are Arabs. Many Muslims are religious. They pray five times a day. The call to prayer is sung from the tower of every mosque. Muslims also consider Jerusalem a holy city, but they pray toward Mecca in Saudi Arabia. They do not pray toward Jerusalem as Jews do.

Judaism, Christianity, and Islam all think of Jerusalem as a holy city. What does this do to everyday life in the city?

_____

_____

_____

How can each group show respect for the others?

_____

_____

_____

_____

The Druze are a peaceful people. They are Arabs. Their religion is not Christianity. It is not Islam. Their religion is secret. They do not share it with outsiders. The Druze speak Arabic, but they are not part of the mainstream Arab community. In the War of Independence in 1948, the Druze fought with the Jews against the Arabs.

IBRAHIM

Bedouin are the wanderers of Israel. They usually live in tents. They can pick up their things and move quickly. They move from place to place to find food and water for their flocks. They raise goats, sheep, and camels. Some Bedouin now live in houses. They also serve in the Israeli army. They are known for their tracking skills. This means that they are able to follow and find enemies very well. They are able to move about quietly and almost unseen.

Help the tracker move across the desert to see what those on the other side are doing.

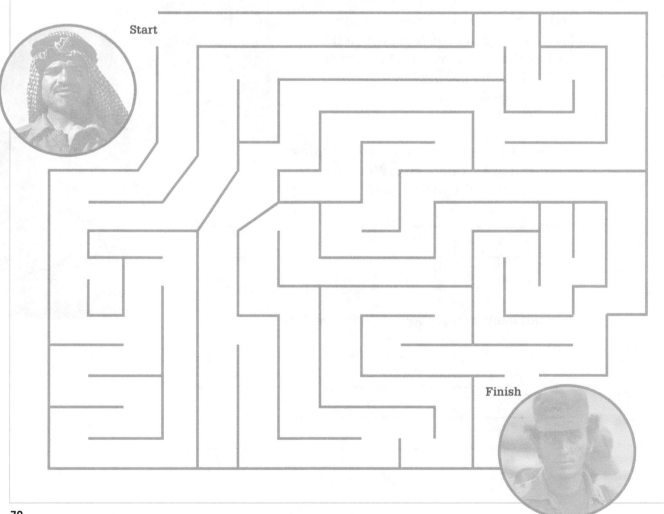

Start

Finish

Why should we know about people in Israel other than Jews? The Torah says: "You shall not wrong a stranger or oppress him, for you were strangers in the land of Egypt." (In the Torah, "stranger" means someone from another place. It does not just mean someone you do not know.) What do you think these words from the Torah mean?

_____

How do these words fit life in Israel?

_____

How do they fit life in your hometown?

_____

Find a short newspaper or magazine article about different cultures or groups living in Israel. Paste it on this page. Read the article. Read the headline again. Make up a better headline for the article.

Original Headline: _____

Improved Headline: _____

Which headline tells what the article is about in a better way?

_____

Which is more likely to make someone want to read the article? Why?

_____

_____

ALON

You have learned a lot about our Homeland from my friends and me. Can you list three things you have learned?

_____

_____

_____

Can you list one thing that surprised you?

_____

Many things in Israel are different from those in your community. Many things are the same. On the next two pages, circle the things that are the same. Put a square around those that are different.

DAILY ROUTINE

School

Visiting the Kotel

Sports

FAMILY DAYS

Restaurant

Zoo

Museum

SHOPPING

Olive Stand

Shopping Mall

Outdoor Market

VACATIONS

Fishing

Beach

Camel Ride

Listen to several tapes or CDs. Find music that would best "describe" daily life in Israel. List the names of the songs.

Song Titles:

1. _____

2. _____

3. _____

4. _____

Using parts of the songs listed above, prepare a tape to form a "Homeland Medley."

ALON

MICHAL

SHMUEL

YAEL

OREN

RONIT

IBRAHIM

You have seen our country. Now it is time to learn "Hatikvah." That is the national anthem of Israel and the Jewish people.

כָּל עוֹד בַּלֵּבָב פְּנִימָה	Kol od balevav penimah
נֶפֶשׁ יְהוּדִי הוֹמִיָּה	Nefesh yehudi homiyah
וּלְפַאֲתֵי מִזְרָח קָדִימָה	Ulefa'atey mizrach kadimah
עַיִן לְצִיּוֹן צוֹפִיָּה	Ayin leTziyon tzofiyah
עוֹד לֹא אָבְדָה תִּקְוָתֵנוּ	Od lo avdah tikvatenu
הַתִּקְוָה בַּת שְׁנוֹת אַלְפַּיִם	Hatikvah bat sh'not alpayim
לִהְיוֹת עַם חָפְשִׁי בְּאַרְצֵנוּ	Lih'yot am chofshi be'artzenu
אֶרֶץ צִיּוֹן וִירוּשָׁלַיִם.	Eretz Tzion virushalayim.

(So long as still within our breasts
The Jewish heart beats true,
So long as still towards the East,
To Zion, looks the Jew,
So long our hopes are not yet lost —
Two thousand years we cherished them —
To live in freedom in the land
Of Zion and Jerusalem.)

Learn to sing "Hatikvah." Think about the meaning of the words when you sing them.
What do you feel when you hear or sing your country's national anthem?

_____

_____

What do you feel when you hear or sing "Hatikvah," the national anthem of your Homeland?

_____

_____

Speak with your relatives and friends to find out what they feel when they hear or sing "Hatikvah."

Look through the notebook you made about the seven Israeli guides. Compare the life of each of them with your own life. How are their lives the same as yours? How are they different from yours?

SAME

_____

_____

_____

_____

_____

_____

DIFFERENT

_____

_____

_____

_____

_____

Draw a picture or write a few lines about something that makes you feel connected to Israel. It might be a place. It might be an activity. It could even be a special person. Tell why you chose it.

We hope you have enjoyed our tour of the Land of Israel, our Home and our Homeland. We have enjoyed getting to know you. Always remember that we are all part of the people of Israel.

As the Talmud says, "All Israel are friends. We will always be connected to each other and to Israel."

Below, make a list of things that would make a good bulletin board about your connections to Israel. Together with your classmates, create the bulletin board. Call it *K'sharim*. That means "connections." Add to it whenever you find something interesting about Israel. This will help you remember us and our country.

_____

_____

_____

_____

_____

_____

Shalom u'lehitraot. Good-bye for now.
We hope you will come and visit us soon.

Love,
Michal, Ronit, Yael, Alon, Oren,
Shmuel, and Ibrahim